CONSTRUCTING WALKING JAZZ

STANDARD LINES

A COMPREHENSIVE GUIDE TO CONSTRUCTING WALKING JAZZ BASS LINES

FOR THE

ELECTRIC BASS

BASS TAB
EDITION

COMPILED AND COMPOSED
BY
STEVEN MOONEY

Cover Design by Steven Mooney

©Waterfall Publishing House 2011

Special thanks to Jimmy Vass, Darcy Wright and Charlie Banacos
and to my wife Madoka for her constant love and support.

Print Edition ISBN 978-1-937187-15-6
Ebook   ISBN 978-1-937187-16-3

Library of Congress Control Number: 2011928126

Musical Score : Jazz
Musical Score : Studies & exercises, etudes

Layout and music engraving by Steven Mooney
Cover Design by Steven Mooney

FOREWARD

Standard Lines Book III in the Constructing Walking Jazz Bass Lines series for the Electric Bassist is a comprehensive guide demonstrating the devices used to construct walking jazz bass lines in the jazz standard tradition.

Book III covers 24 standard jazz chord progressions with 110 choruses of professional jazz bass lines as an example.

Part I outlines the Modes and the chord scale relationships and the fundamental knowledge required to be able to build the diatonic triads and 7th chords in any key. Examples are given in the " 2 " feel and " 4 " feel walking bass style enabling the bassist to develop a strong rhythmic and harmonic foundation.

More advanced bass line construction examples including voice leading and mode substitutions and mode applications related to specific jazz chord progressions are also outlined.

Part II outlines the Symmetric Scales as well as the Modes of the Melodic Minor Scale related to the Minor II V I progression. Provided are written examples of the Symmetric Scales and the chord scale relationships and how to apply the use of the Symmetric Scales over popular jazz chord progressions.

The Minor II V I is outlined and compared to the Major II V I outlining the differences with the suggested scale uses applied to common jazz chord progressions.

Part III outlines the use of the BeBop Scales and their use in the jazz walking bass tradition, providing suggested uses of the BeBop scales related to popular jazz chord progressions.

Part IV outlines the previous lesson devices and concepts with examples of professional level bass lines over standard jazz chord progressions.

All information builds in a stepwise progression enabling the bassist to apply the techniques in all 12 keys.

TABLE OF CONTENTS

TABLE OF CONTENTS

TABLE OF CONTENTS

TABLE OF CONTENTS

PART I THE CHORD SCALE RELATIONSHIPS

HOW TO APPLY THE MODES AND THE CHORD/SCALE RELATIONSHIPS TO STANDARD JAZZ CHORD PROGRESSIONS.

Having a working knowledge of the modes and the chord /scale relationships enables the bassist a to develop a stronger awareness of the chord structure or harmony being played.

As an example, when a bassist sees a chord chart for the first time do they see Amin7 D7 for one measure then Gmin7 C7 going to Fmaj7.
Or are they looking at a III VI II V in the key of F ?
Being able to identify the key centers and how the modes and or chord / scale relationships work, enables a bassist to analyse and memorise a tune much easier than thinking of each individual chord.
It will also enable the bassist to transpose the tune into any key on the bandstand.

The first chapter illustrates the modes and their related chord scales and arpeggios over 2 octaves in the key of F major.

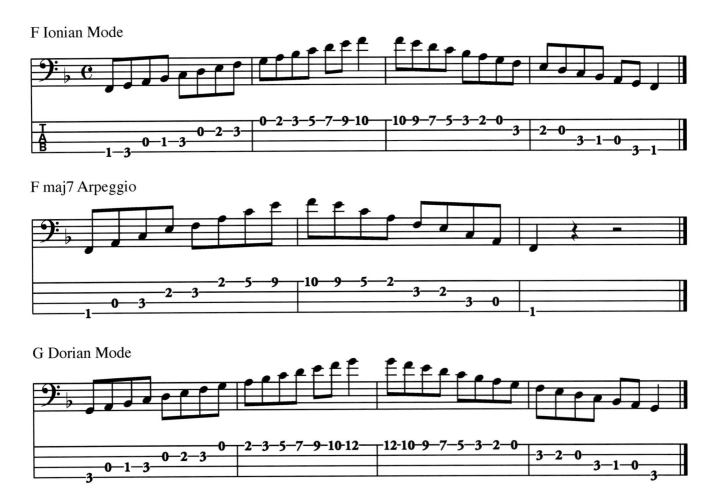

F Ionian Mode

F maj7 Arpeggio

G Dorian Mode

11

G min7 Arpeggio

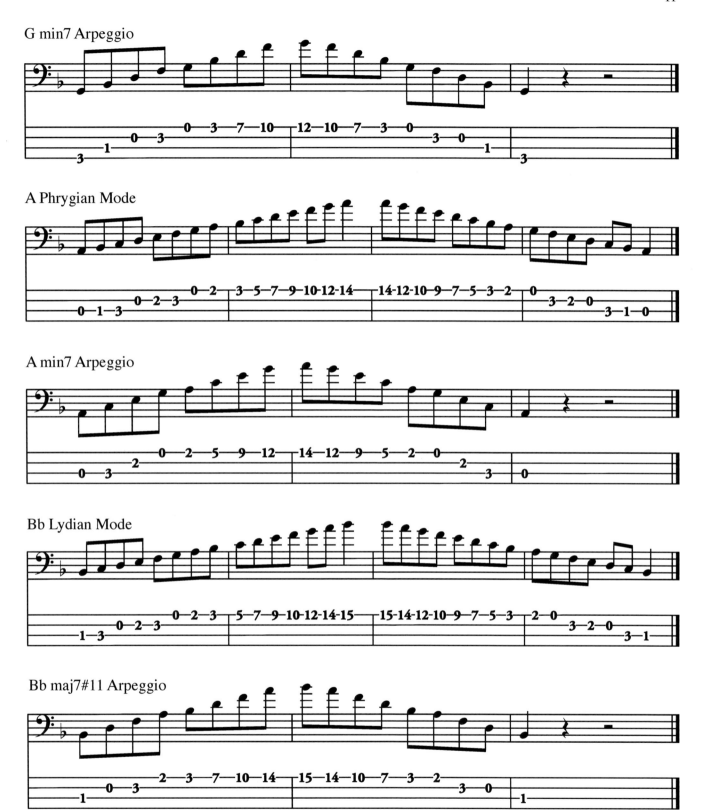

A Phrygian Mode

A min7 Arpeggio

Bb Lydian Mode

Bb maj7#11 Arpeggio

C Mixolydian Mode

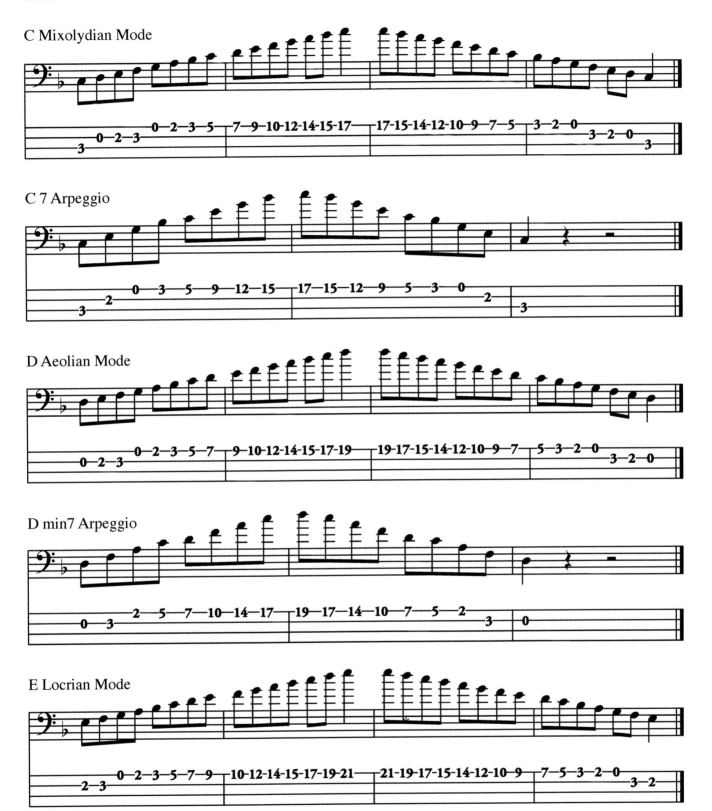

C 7 Arpeggio

D Aeolian Mode

D min7 Arpeggio

E Locrian Mode

E Half diminished Arpeggio

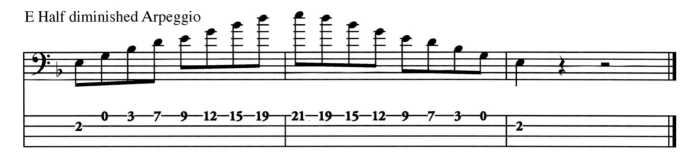

Part I   THE CHORD SCALE RELATIONSHIPS

How To Construct the triads off of the Major scale.

The example below outlines how to construct the diatonic triads off of the major scale
and is the first step in understanding the modes and applying them to *Key Centers*.
The use of triads when constructing walking jazz bass lines has many advantages and
enables the bassist to work on several areas at once.
Firstly the triads outline the changes, by having the triad in the bottom register the
guitarist or pianist can lay the chord extensions on the top, while the soloist gets a strong
foundation of the harmony in the bottom register, giving depth to the overall sound of
the band.
Secondly by playing the triads in the bottom register of the instrument you are working
on building strength and stamina in your fretting hand.
Thirdly, for the fretless electric bassist playing the triads in the bottom register of the
instrument is an excellent exercise for improving intonation. Being able
to walk the lines to a blues or standard chord progression in any key without moving
more than a half step from the open position is something to aspire to.

To construct the triad we start on any given note in the scale and move two steps.
eg F, A, C / G, Bb, D / A, C, E etc.

Ex. 1   F major scale 1 octave.

Ex. 2 The diatonic triads in the key of F major constructed from the F major scale.

* The V triad becomes dominant when the b7th is added.

" PERIODIC "

The example below outlines a fundamental " 2 Feel " bass line played in the bottom register of the instrument constructed entirely from triads. Notes 1, 3, 5 of the chord.

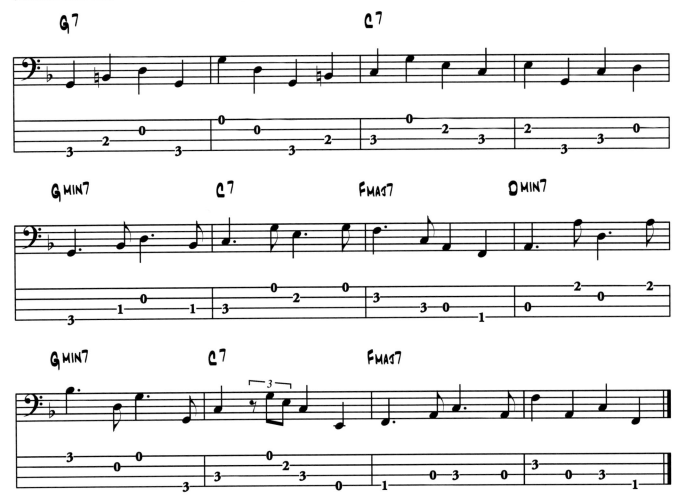

Example 2 outlines the previous standard chord progression " Periodic " using the 4 feel
or walking bass line using the triads to construct the bass line.

17

TRIADS & THE CHROMATIC APPROACH FROM ABOVE

The next example outlines the use of the harmonic device known as the chromatic approach note from above.

The chromatic approach note is used to give the walking bass line contour and a sense of tension and release as the chromatic approach note resolves into the chord tone.

The chromatic approach notes can also be used to keep the chord tones on the down beats eg beats 1 & 3.

The example below shows the " 2 feel " bass line using the triad and the chromatic approach from above.

The next example outlines the walking bass line or " 4 " feel constructed using triads and the chromatic approach from above.

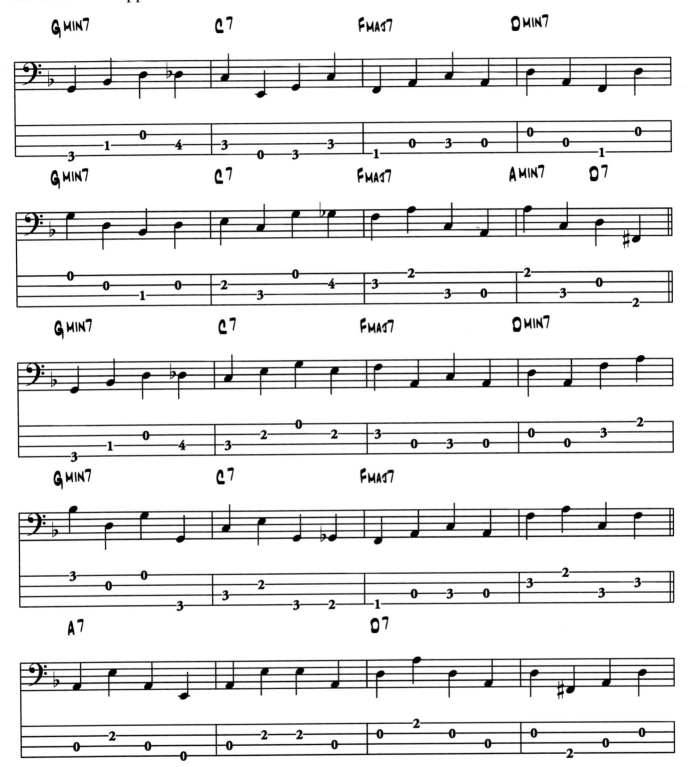

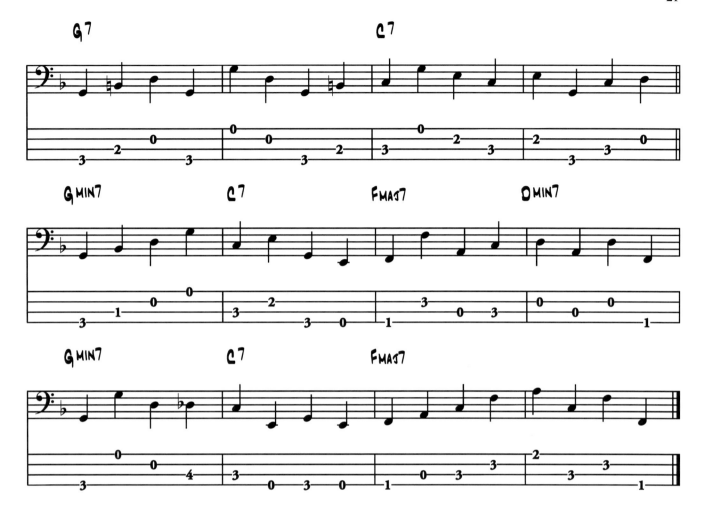

TRIADS & THE CHROMATIC APPROACH FROM BELOW

The next example shows the use of the harmonic device known as the chromatic approach note from a below.

The chromatic approach note is used to give the walking bass line contour and a sense of tension and release as a non diatonic eg. not from the scale, note is used to create the tension and release effect as the chromatic note resolves to the chord tone.

The chromatic approach notes can also be used to keep the chord tones on the down beats eg beats 1 & 3.

The example below shows the " 2 feel " bass line using the triad and the chromatic approach from below.

TRIADS AND THE WALK UP

The next common walking bass device is known as the walk up and describes the method of walking up to the next chord change using two approach notes.

The 1st measure of the 1st A section shows the walk up and there is a variation of the walk up used in the 6th measure on the C7 chord, where the chromatic note is used on the 2nd beat between the C and D.

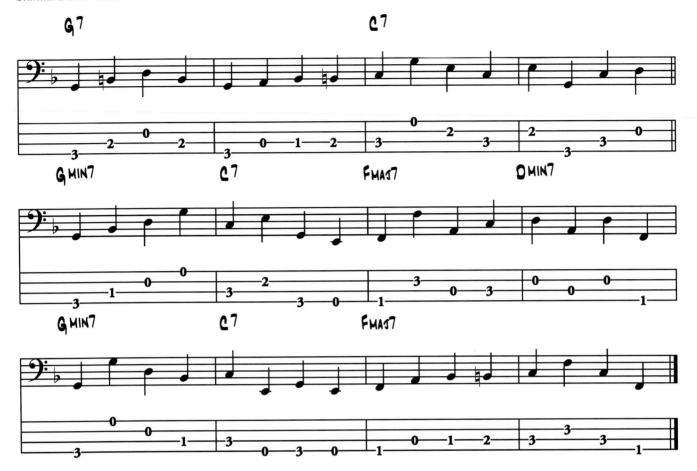

TRIADS AND THE WALK DOWN

The next common walking bass device is known as the walk down and describes the method of walking down to the next chord change using two approach notes.

The 2nd measure of the 2nd A and last A section shows the walk down.

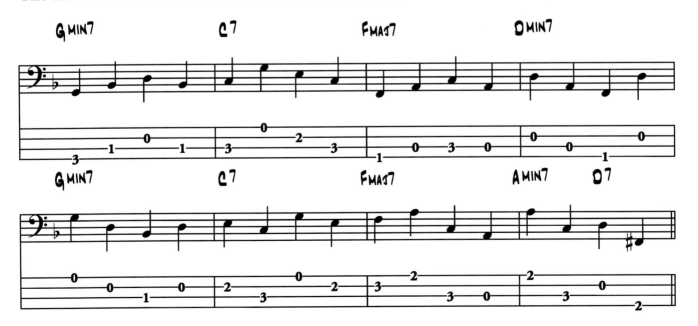

" GREATEST GLOVE "   Jazz chord progression #2

SCALAR APPROACHES TO CONSTRUCTING JAZZ BASS LINES " ASCENDING "

The scalar approach to walking bass lines is a more horizontal approach to constructing bass lines and can give the bass line a smoother contour. Instead of using the triad to construct our line, in this example we construct the line using the scale tones 1235 or a permutation of the 1235 scale tones and also use the triad for variation.
The example below shows the walking bass line or " 4 " feel.

APPLYING 7TH CHORDS TO SCALAR BASS LINES

HOW TO CONSTRUCT THE DIATONIC 7THS

The next example shows the descending approach to constructing scalar bass lines using the 7th chords.

The examples below show how to construct the 7th chords from the major scale.

Ex. the Bb major scale

Ex. 2 The Diatonic Triads constructed from the Bb major scale

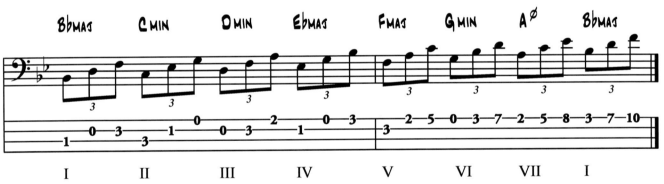

Ex. 3 The diatonic 7th chords constructed from the Bb major scale.

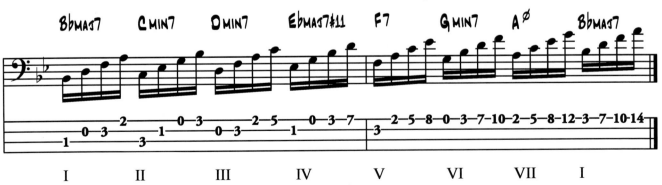

APPLYING 7TH CHORDS TO SCALAR JAZZ BASS LINES " DESCENDING "

The next example shows the use of the scalar approach to construct descending bass lines
using the notes of the scale descending from the root note. (scale tones 1765)
The example also uses the devices of the triads and ascending scalar approaches.
As the examples progress the bass line contours become more varied and tell more of a
melodic story by outlining different notes of the harmony.

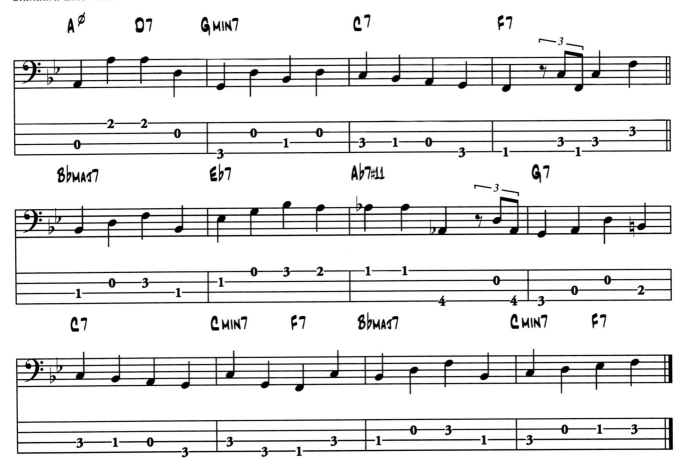

ASCENDING SCALAR WITH CHROMATIC APPROACH FROM ABOVE

The following example outlines the use of the ascending scalar walking bass line combined with the harmonic device the chromatic approach note from above.

DESCENDING SCALAR WITH CHROMATIC APPROACH FROM BELOW

The following example outlines the use of the descending scalar walking bass line combined with the harmonic device the chromatic approach note from below.

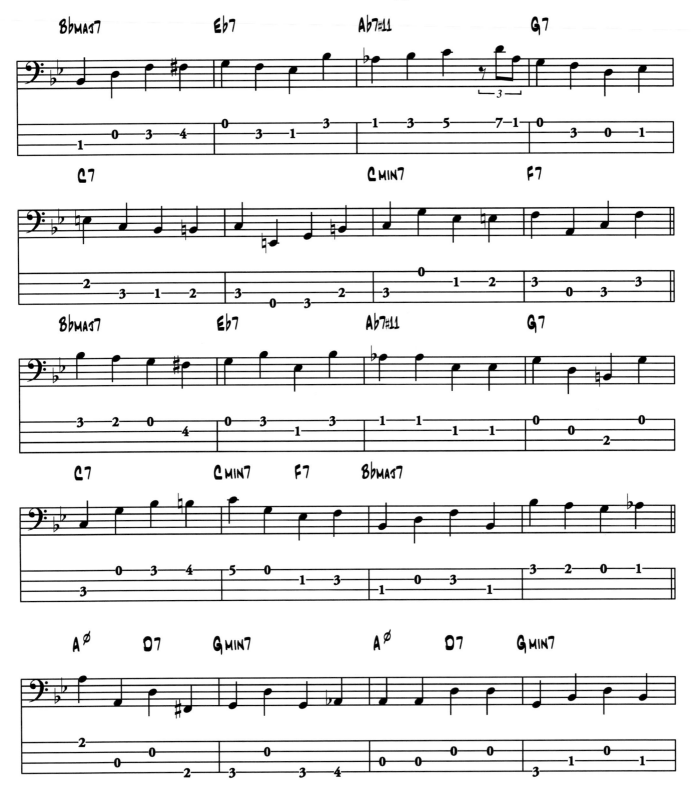

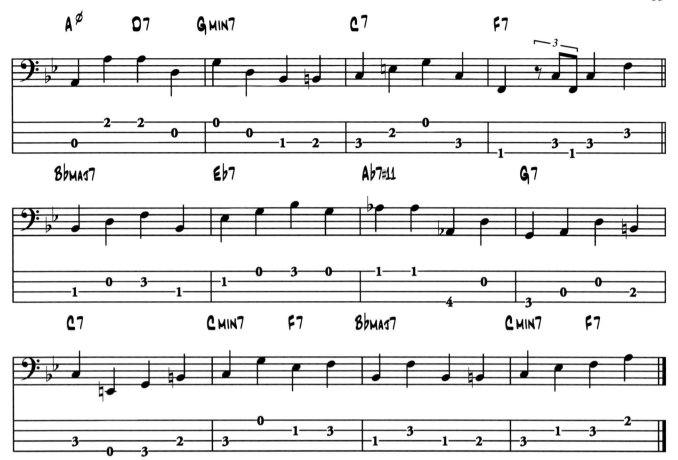

VOICE LEADING 7th CHORDS & THE II V I PROGRESSION

In the following example we incorporate 7th chords and the technique of voice leading into our II V I progression.

The voice leading technique will be used to link the IImin7 chord to the V7 chord. Voice leading is a very effective technique used by all harmonic instruments.

By using the voice leading technique shown below the bass lines are now connected to how the pianist or guitarist may voice the chords.

Ex. 1 shows the II V I progression in the key of Bb major

Ex. 2 shows the voice leading technique, here the Bb the b7th of Cmin7 resolves down a half step to the A the major 3rd of F7.

Ex. 3 shows the voice leading technique, here the Bb the b7th of Cmin7 resolves up a whole step to the C the 5th of F7.

" WINTERS COMING "   Jazz chord progression # 3

APPLYING THE VOICE LEADING TECHNIQUE TO JAZZ BASS LINES

VOICE LEADING THE DOMINANT 7TH CHORD

The next chapter outlines the voice leading principle applied to the Dominant 7th chord. The term voice leading means moving a chord tone stepwise to another chord tone of the next chord change.
The following examples outline the voice leading principle in the key of Bb major.

The first example outlines the II V I progression in the key of Bb major. The bass line does not use the voice leading principle on the F7 chord.

This will enable the bassist to hear the difference between the examples.

Ex. 1

Ex. 2 The voice leading technique is used in the 2nd measure on the F7 chord, here the Eb the b7th of F7 moves down a half step to D the major 3rd of the Bb major chord.

Ex. 3 The voice leading technique is used in the 2nd measure on the F7 chord, here the Eb the b7th of F7 moves up a whole step to F the 5th of Bb major.

By using the voice leading techniques the bass lines connect with a stronger sense of forward motion and are now linked to the way the chordal instruments may voice the chords.

The following example bass lines on " Winters Coming " use the voice leading principle on the F7 chord.

" WINTERS COMING "   Jazz chord progression #3

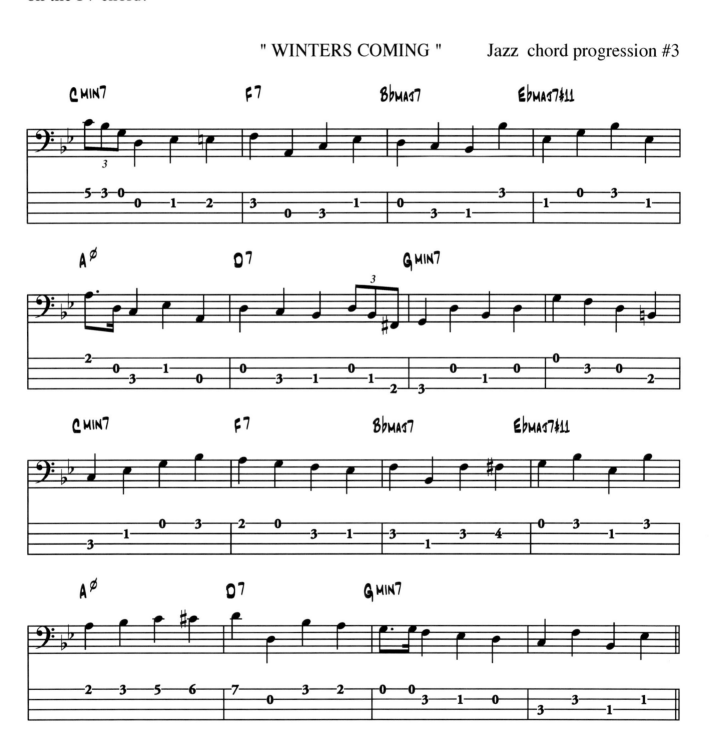

Standard Line Vol.I

HOW TO APPLY THE MODES TO CONSTRUCTING WALKING JAZZ BASS LINES

The next chapter outlines the use of using the modes to construct walking bass lines and how to identify the use of the chord scale relationships in jazz functional harmony.

The first chapter outlined the modes and the related scales and arpeggios, and how to construct the modes off of the Major scale.

By being able to identify the chord structure or how the chords are functioning eg, I V I, or II V I, I VI II V etc enables the bassist to apply the use of the modes and the chord scale relationships.

By applying the use of the Modes to *key centers* the bassist can then construct longer lines outlining the key and move away from playing bass lines which outline 1 chord per measure.

The result is a different bass melody or story. Both approaches outline the changes and are valid methods of playing the changes.

The bassist should equip themselves with as many choices as possible. The result is more freedom to apply different bass melodies and to provide varying inspiration to the soloist.

The IONIAN MODE or the I MAJOR CHORD

The next standard jazz chord progression " Mr K " outlines the application of the Ionian Mode or I maj chord in the key of F major.

The F Ionian Mode

The F major 7 arpeggio

" MR. K " Jazz chord progression # 4

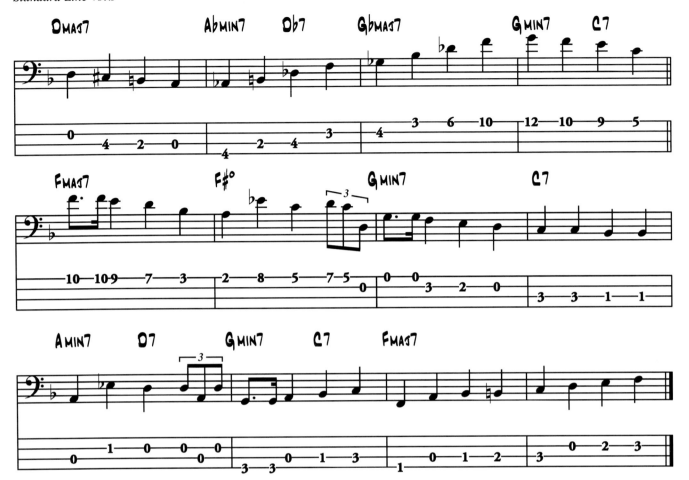

THE MAJOR II V I PROGRESSION AND THE DORIAN & MIXOLYDIAN MODES

The next example shows the application of the Dorian and Mixolydian modes when constructing bass lines.

The standard chord progression # 4 " Mr K " in the key of F major outlines the use of the Dorian and Mixolydian modes when walking over the II V I progression.

The examples below show the related Dorian and Mixolydian modes from the key of F major.

The G Dorian scale

G min7 2 octave arpeggio

The C Mixolydian scale

The C7 2 octave arpeggio

THE II V I PROGRESSION

The following chapter outlines the II V I progression and its function in jazz harmony.
The II V I progression or the II V is one of the most commonly used cycles in the jazz
standard repertoire and should be learnt in all 12 keys.
By refering again to the diatonic 7ths in F major we see where the II V I language is from.
The term II V I refers to the second chord in the scale the II minor7 chord followed by the
fifth chord in the scale the Dominant 7th chord.
The Dominant 7th chord wants to resolve, which brings us back to the root or the I chord in
the scale, the II V I cycle is completed.

The Diatonic 7th Chords in the key of F major.

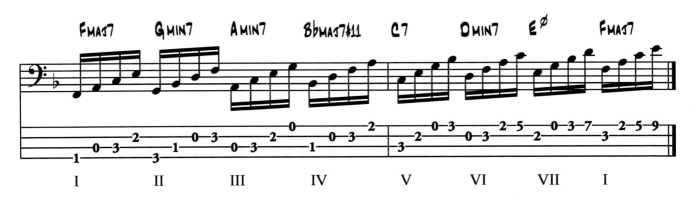

Below is an example of the II V I progression in the key of F major using triads.

Below is an example of the II V I progression in the key of F major using the scalar approach
to constructing bass lines.

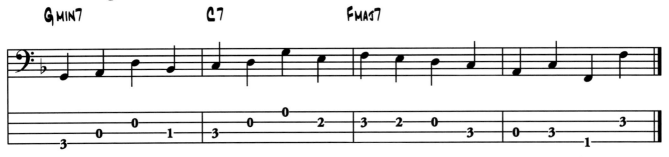

THE APPLICATION OF THE II V PROGRESSION IN JAZZ CHORD PROGRESSIONS

The next example shows the standard chord progression " Mr K " outlining the II V I progression in the key of F major using the " 2 Feel " bass line.

Notice in measures 3 and 4 and the 7th and 8th measures of the 1st A section we have the II V progression. The 2nd A has a II V leading to the Bb major, the first chord of the bridge or B section.

In the first A we use the triadic approach to construct the walking bass line over the II V progression, in the 2nd A and Last A we use the scalar approach to construct the walking bass line over the II V progression.

THE III VI II V PROGRESSION AND THE PHYRGIAN MODE

Below is an example of the diatonic 7th chords in the key of F major.

By refering to the diatonic 7th charts we can see where the III VI II V progression comes from.

Notice that in this example the VI chord is a Dominant 7th chord. This is because the VI chord D7 is functioning as a Secondary Dominant chord.

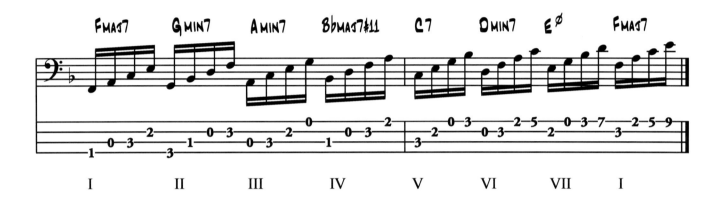

A Phrygian mode or III chord

A min7 2 octave arpeggio

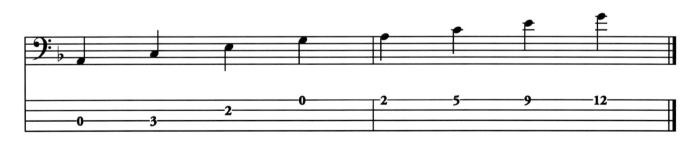

** Secondary Dominant chords are discussed in more detail in book II and IV

III VI II V PROGRESSION

In the following chapter we will look at the III VI II V progression and its function in jazz chord progressions.

Like the II V I progression or the II V the III VI II V is one of the most commonly used cycles in the jazz standard repertoire and should be learnt in all 12 keys.

By refering again to the diatonic 7ths in F major we see where the III VI II V language is from.

The term III VI II V I refers to the 3rd chord the III min7, the 6th chord the VImin7 or its substitute the VI 7 chord, the second chord in the scale the II minor 7 chord followed by the fifth chord in the scale the Dominant 7th chord.

The Dominant 7th chord wants to resolve, which brings us to the root or the I chord in the scale, the III VI II V I cycle is completed.

Below is an example of the III VI II V I progression in the key of F major using the triadic approach to construct the walking bass line.

Below is an example of the III VI II V I progression in the key of F major using the scalar approach to construct the walking bass line.

THE APPLICATION OF THE III VI II V PROGRESSION IN JAZZ CHORD PROGRESSIONS

The next example outlines jazz chord progression # 4 " MR. K "

Notice in the measures 5 - 8 of the first A we have the III VI II V progression.
In the Last A we have the III VI II V progression over 2 bars in measures 5 - 6.

Notice in bar 1 & 2 of the 2nd A, the descending A Phrygian scale is played to outline the
F maj 7 chord starting on A, the third of Fmaj 7 and descends through the D min7 chord
onto the G, or root of G min7.

This is an example of substituting the I chord for the III min7 chord or Phrygian scale.

THE I VI II V CHORD PROGRESSION AND THE AEOLIAN MODE

The next progression in this chapter is the I VI II V progression, like the II V I progression the I VI II V progression is one of the most common chord sequences in the standard jazz vocabulary.

By refering to the diatonic 7ths in F major shown below, we can see where the I VI II V language is from.

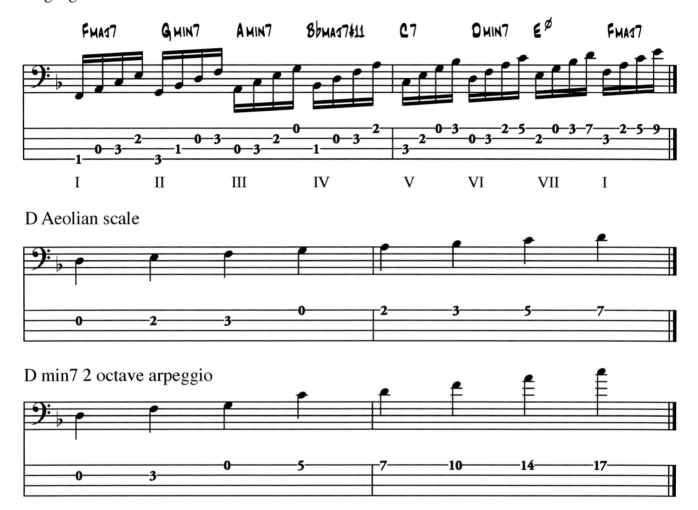

Below is an example of the I VI II V progression in the key of F major using the triadic approach to construct the walking bass line.

Below is an example of the I VI II V I progression in the key of F major using the scalar approach to construct the walking bass line.

Descending I VI II V bass line

Below is an example of the I VI II V progression in the key of F major using the triadic approach to construct the walking bass line.

Below is an example of the I VI II V I progression in the key of F major using the scalar approach to construct the walking bass line.
Notice by using the scalar lines and the modes the lines can move in one direction for an extended number of measures. The A Phrygian scale is played against the Fmaj 7 chord

THE APPLICATION OF THE I VI II V PROGRESSION IN JAZZ CHORD PROGRESSIONS

" MR. K " Jazz chord progression # 4

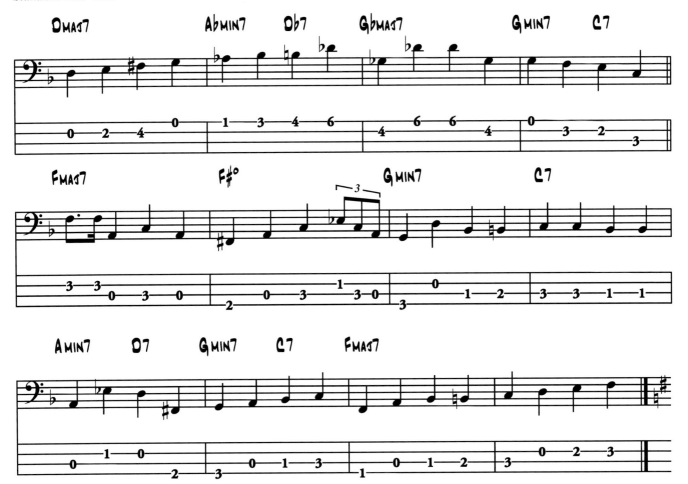

THE LYDIAN MODE

The Lydian Mode is the 4th mode of the major scale and is played against the Maj7 #11 chord.

Starting a tune on the IV major chord or modulating to the IV major chord in the bridge is a very common harmonic device used in functional jazz harmony.

Shown below is the Diatonic 7ths in the key of G major.
By refering to the diatonic 7ths in G major shown below, we can see where the IV maj 7 language comes from.

Ex.1 The C Lydian scale 2 octaves

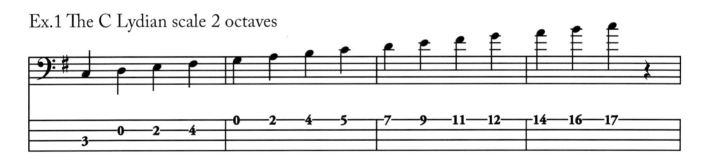

The C maj7 #11 2 octave arpeggio

" IT DEPENDS "   Jazz chord progression # 5

APPLYING THE LYDIAN MODE TO CONSTRUCTING JAZZ BASS LINES

The following jazz progression " IT DEPENDS " starts on the IV major chord and outlines the use of the Lydian scale.

THE LOCRIAN MODE

The Locrian scale is the seventh mode of the Major scale and is played over the Half Diminished chord eg, min7b5.

Shown below is the Diatonic 7ths in the key of C major.

By refering to the diatonic 7ths in C major shown below, we can see where the VII Half Diminished language comes from.

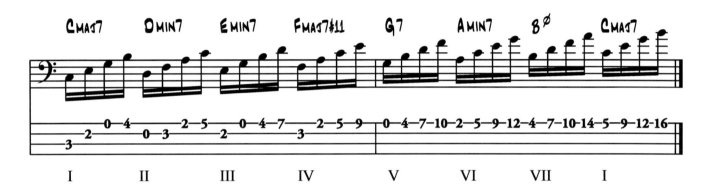

The example below shows the B Locrian scale the 7th mode of the C major scale or the VII Half Diminished chord.

Ex. 1 The B Locrian scale 2 octaves

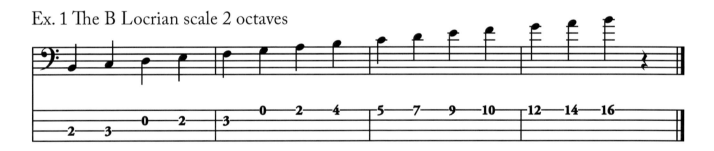

Ex. 2 The B min7b5 arpeggio 2 octaves

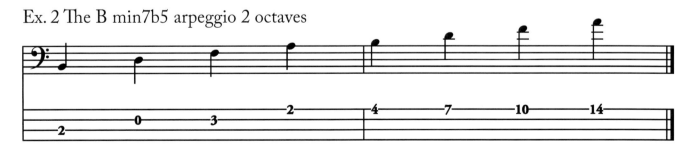

The following jazz chord progression " THE WEAVING STREAM " outlines the use of the VII Half Diminished chord and the Locrian mode in the 3rd measure of the first and second half of the tune.

" THE WEAVING STREAM "   Jazz chord progression # 6

APPLYING THE LOCRIAN MODE TO CONSTRUCTING JAZZ BASS LINES

71

©Waterfall Publishing House 2011

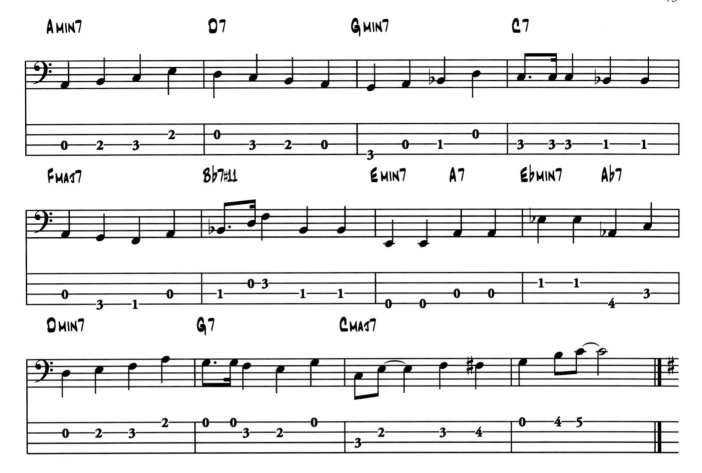

Part II   SYMMETRIC & MELODIC MINOR SCALES

Part II of the Book outlines the use of the Symmetric scales and the Modes of the Melodic Minor scale used to construct walking jazz bass lines in the standard jazz repertoire.

So far we have looked at the scales and modes derived from the Major scale.

In this next section of the book we look at what are known as the Symmetric scales.

The Whole tone scale

The Diminished scale (whole, half)

The Diminished scale (half, whole).

As well as the scales often used to play over the Minor II V I progression derived from the Melodic Minor scale.

The Altered scale

The Locrian #2 scale.

Melodic Minor scale. (Jazz)

In this chapter we discuss the use of the ascending Melodic Minor scale, which is often used in the jazz vocabulary.
In classical music the Melodic Minor uses a different scale construction when descending eg (b6th and b7th).

THE WHOLE TONE SCALE

The Whole tone scale is a Symmetric scale, meaning the intervals have a consistant pattern, eg whole steps or tones, which is where the term whole tone scale comes from. The Whole tone scale is a 6 note scale with a very distinctive sound and is often played over the Dom 7 #5 chord or the Dom 7 b5 chord. Because of the whole tone construction of the scale there are only 2 Whole tone scales, all other Whole tone scales are built from these two scales. The following jazz AABA chord progression applies the use of the Whole tone scale in measures 3 - 4 of the A sections over the D7 b5 chord.

Ex 1 The D Whole tone scale

Ex 2 The D7#5 2 octave arpeggio

" WHERES THE SUBWAY "   Jazz chord progression # 7
APPLYING THE WHOLE TONE SCALE TO CONSTRUCTING JAZZ BASS LINES

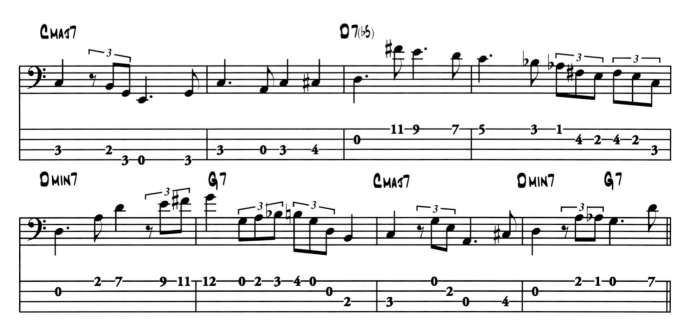

83

THE DIMINISHED SCALE

The Diminished scale is another of the Symmetric scales and contains 8 notes, consisting of the whole step half step pattern of intervals. The Diminished scale is played over the Diminished 7 chord.

Because of the symmetric pattern of intervals there are only 3 Diminished scales.

Ex.1 The Ab Diminished scale 2 octaves

The Ab Diminished arpeggio 2 octaves

By building the Diminished scale off of the degrees of the scale a minor 3rd apart and using the whole step half step formula we arrive at the 4 Diminished scales built from the same scale. Ab, B, D and F Diminished scales are the same scale starting on a different note.

By moving up a half step from Ab we can build the A, C, Eb and Gb Diminished scales.

By moving up a half step from A we can build the Bb, Db, E and G Diminished scales.

The example below shows the A Diminished scale.

The example below shows the Bb Diminished scale.

The following jazz progression " FINDING CANDY " outlines the use of the diminished scale in the 2nd and 6th measure of the first and second half of the tune.

" FINDING CANDY "   Jazz chord progression # 8

APPLYING THE DIMINISHED SCALE TO CONSTRUCTING JAZZ BASS LINES

THE HALF WHOLE DIMINISHED SCALE

The Half whole diminished scale is another of the Symmetric scales and contains 8 notes and consists of the half step, whole step pattern of intervals.

The H/W diminished scale is often played over the Dominant 7b9 chord.

Because of the symmetric pattern of intervals there are only 3 H/W diminished scales.

The example shown below is the C Half whole step diminished scale.

The C Half whole step diminished scale is the same as the Bb Whole step half step diminished scale.

The C Half whole diminished scale

The C7 b9 2 octave arpeggio

By building the H/W diminished scale off of the degrees of the scale a minor 3rd apart and using the half step whole step half step formula we arrive at the 4 diminished scales built from the same scale. Ab, B, D and F Half whole diminished scales are the same scale starting on a different note.

By moving up a half step from Ab we can build the A, C, Eb and Gb H/W diminished scales.

By moving up a half step from A we can build the Bb, Db, E and G H/W diminished scales.

The example below shows the A H/W diminished scale.

The example below shows the Bb H/W diminished scale.

The following jazz progression " VEGETABLE STEW " uses the ABCD formula with four 8 measure sections.

The use of the Half whole diminished scale is used over the C7b9 chord in the second measure of the A B and D sections.

" VEGETABLE STEW "   Jazz chord progression # 9

APPLYING THE HALF WHOLE DIMINISHED SCALE TO CONSTRUCTING JAZZ BASS LINES

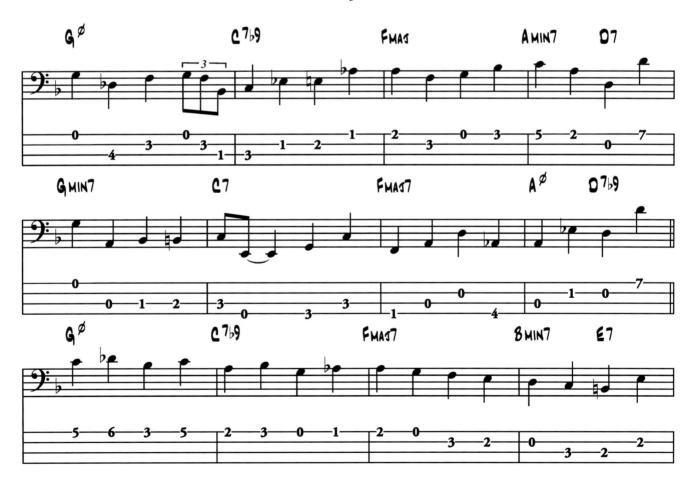

THE DIMINISHED WHOLE TONE SCALE & THE MINOR II V PROGRESSION

The Diminished whole tone scale is the 7th mode of the Melodic Minor scale and is played over the Altered 7th chord.

The scale starts like a Diminished scale and ends like a Whole tone scale, and is where the term Dimished whole tone comes from.

The Diminished whole tone scale functions as the V chord in a Minor II V I progression.

Ex.1 The Bb Melodic Minor scale *

Ex.2 The A Diminished whole tone scale 2 octaves

Ex.3 The A Altered 2 octave arpeggio

* Notice that the Melodic Minor scale is constructed using a major 7th. The scale is like a major scale using a minor 3rd instead of the major 3rd.

" MOONLIGHT VIEW "   Jazz chord progression # 10

APPLYING THE DIMINISHED WHOLE TONE SCALE TO CONSTRUCTING JAZZ BASS LINES

101

THE LOCRIAN #2 MODE AND THE MINOR II V PROGRESSION

The Locrian #2 or the Super Locrian scale is the 6th mode of the Melodic Minor scale and is played over the Min7 b5 chord and functions as the II chord in a Minor II V I progression.

Ex. 1 The G Melodic Minor scale

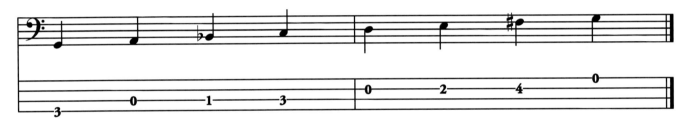

Ex.2 The E Locrian #2 scale

Ex. 3 The E min7b5 arpeggio

" MOONLIGHT VIEW "   Jazz chord progression # 10

APPLYING THE LOCRIAN #2 SCALE TO CONSTRUCTING JAZZ BASS LINES

THE MINOR II V PROGRESSION.

In the previous examples we looked at the Minor II V I progression. The next examples outline the difference between the Min II V I progression and the II V I in a Major key.

The II V I in major uses the Dorian, Mixolydian scales to construct the walking bass lines over the II V I progression. The progression stays in the same key.

The Minor II V I progression uses the Locrian #2 and the Diminished whole tone scales to construct the walking bass lines over the II V I progression.
The difference is the Locrian #2 and the Diminished whole tone scales used to outline the Minor II V I progression are from different keys.

As an example the II V I in C Major is shown below.

The II V I progression in C Major uses the D Dorian scale , G Mixolydian scale and resolves to the C Major scale. All the scales used are modes from the C Major scale, the

progression is in the key of C Major for 4 measures.

The next example shows the Minor II V I progression in the key of C Minor

In this example The Minor II V I moves through 3 keys. The Dmin7b5 chord is the 6th modeof the F Melodic Minor scale.
The G Alt chord is the 7th mode of the Ab Melodic Minor scale.
The C Min maj7 chord is the I chord or Tonic Minor from the C Melodic Minor scale.

The examples below outline the chord scales used in the Minor II V I progression and their related keys.

Ex. 1 F Melodic Minor scale

The D Locrian #2 scale the II Chord in the Minor II V I in C Minor

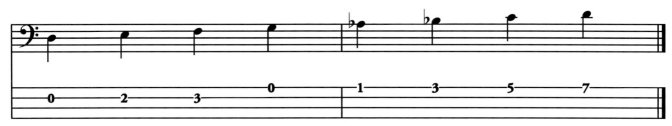

Ex. 2 Ab Melodic Minor scale

The G Altered scale the V chord in the Minor II V I in C Minor

Ex. 3 The C Melodic Minor scale

The C Minor maj 7 scale or the Tonic Minor, the I chord in the Minor II V I in C Minor

Part III   THE BE BOP SCALES

THE ASCENDING MAJOR BEBOP SCALE

The Bebop scales are scales containing an additional chromatic passing tone used to give the line forward motion and are used in walking bass lines and also in improvising.
The chromatic passing tone helps to outline the harmony over an extended line using the same scale.

Example 1 shows the ascending Eb Major scale over two octaves.

Notice when we get to the second octave or beat 1 of the 3rd measure the first beat of the bar or the *down beat* is F and the next down beat, beat 3 of the 3rd measure is Ab, the *avoid* note in the Eb Major scale.

Whats being outlined is F Minor, not Eb Major.

The avoid note? By avoid note we mean it is advisable not to use the 4th note of the major scale on a down beat against a Major chord. This is because of the semi tone clash between the major 3rd of the chord and the 4th note of the scale.

Eb Major scale ascending 2 octaves, beats 1 & 3 are the down beats.

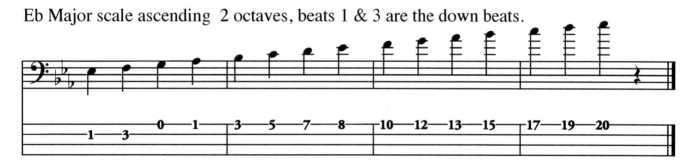

In example 2 we have the Eb Major Bebop scale over 2 octaves ascending.
Notice now by adding the chromatic passing tone B natural or the b6th degree of the scale we now have stronger forward motion over the extended line.
Now all the down beats contain the chord tones, outlining the harmony very clearly and giving a stronger sense of where the line is going.

Eb Major Bebop scale ascending 2 octaves, beats 1 & 3 are the down beats.

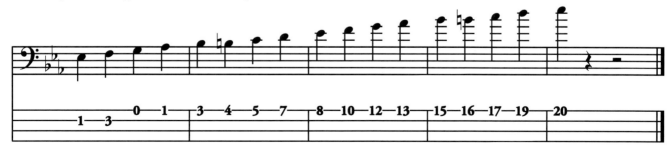

THE DESCENDING MAJOR BEBOP SCALES.

Example 3 shows the descending Eb Major scale over two octaves.

Notice when we get to the second octave or beat 1 of the 3rd measure the first beat of the bar or the *down beat* is D and the next down beat, beat 3 of the 3rd measure is Bb.

Whats being outlined is Bb7, or D Half diminished.

Example 3 Eb Major scale descending 2 octaves, beats 1 & 3 are the down beats.

In example 4 we have the Eb Major Bebop scale over 2 octaves descending.
Notice now by adding the chromatic passing tone B natural or the b6th degree of the scale we now have stronger forward motion over the extended line.
Now all the down beats contain the chord tones, outlining the harmony very clearly and giving a stronger sense of where the line is going.
Notice on beats 1 and 3 in measures 1 and 3 we have the Eb and C natural, this gives the line an Eb Major 6 sound. The down beats over the 4 measure line are Eb, C, Bb, G outlining the Eb Major tonality.

Example 4 Eb Major Bebop scale descending 2 octaves, beats 1 & 3 are the down beats.

In the next example we look at " MORE STEW " jazz chord progression # 11 and apply the use of the Major Bebop scale when constructing our bass line.

* The bottom Eb is out of the range of the standard tuning of the double bass and 4 string electric bass and is used as a musical example only, to demonstrate the explanation of the lesson topic. The note can be played on a 5 string bass or Double bass with C Extension.

"MORE STEW ?" Jazz chord progression # 11

APPLYING THE MAJOR BEBOP SCALE TO CONSTRUCTING JAZZ BASS LINES

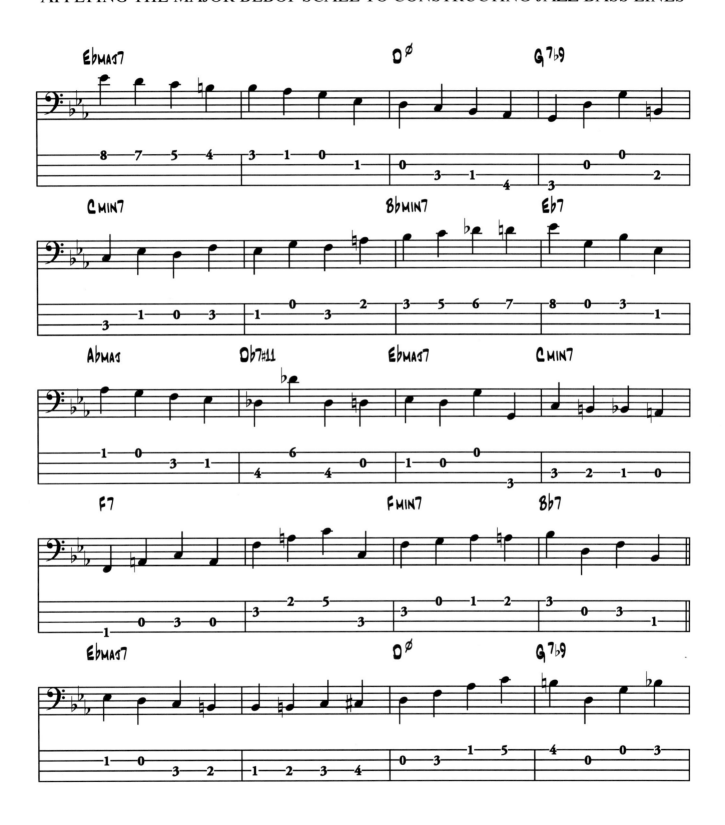

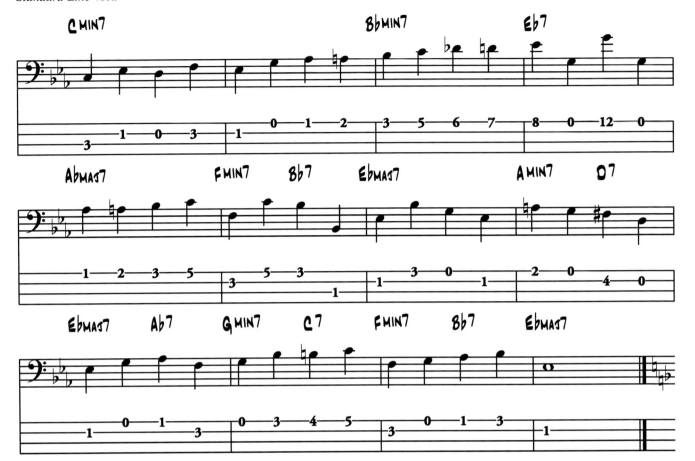

THE ASCENDING DORIAN BEBOP SCALE

The Bebop scales are scales containing an additional chromatic passing tone used to give the line forward motion and are used in walking bass lines and also in improvising.
The chromatic passing tone helps to outline the harmony over an extended line using the same scale.

Example 1 shows the Dorian scale over two octaves.

Notice when we get to the second octave or beat 1 of the 3rd measure the first beat of the bar or the *down beat* is A and the next down beat, beat 3 of the 3rd measure is C.

Whats being outlined is A minor.

G Dorian scale ascending 2 octaves, beats 1 & 3 are the down beats.

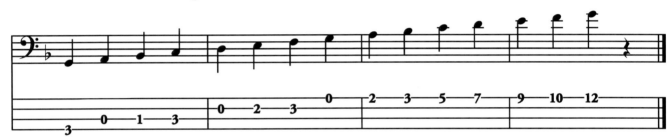

In example 2 we have the G Dorian Bebop scale over 2 octaves ascending.
Notice now by adding the chromatic passing tone F# or the major 7th degree of the scale we now have stronger forward motion over the extended line.
Now all the down beats contain the chord tones, outlining the harmony very clearly and giving a stronger sense of where the line is going.

G Dorian Bebop scale ascending 2 octaves, beats 1 & 3 are the down beats.

THE DESCENDING DORIAN BEBOP SCALE.

Example 3 shows the descending G Dorian scale over two octaves.

Notice when we get to the second octave or beat 1 of the 3rd measure the first beat of the bar or the *down beat* is F and the next down beat, beat 3 of the 3rd measure is D.

Whats being outlined is D min7.

Example 3 G Dorian scale descending 2 octaves, beats 1 & 3 are the down beats.

In example 4 we have the G Dorian Bebop scale over 2 octaves descending.
Notice now by adding the chromatic passing tone F# or the maj 7th degree of the scale we now have stronger forward motion over the extended line.
Now all the down beats contain the chord tones, outlining the harmony very clearly and giving a stronger sense of where the line is going. Now the down beats are G, F, D and Bb clearly outlining the G min7 tonality.

Example 4 G Dorian Bebop scale descending 2 octaves, beats 1 & 3 are the down beats.

In the next example we look at " HEARD IT " jazz chord progression # 12 and apply the use of the Dorian Bebop scale when constructing our bass line.

" HEARD IT "   Jazz chord progression # 12

APPLYING THE DORIAN MINOR BEBOP SCALE TO
CONSTRUCTING JAZZ BASS LINES

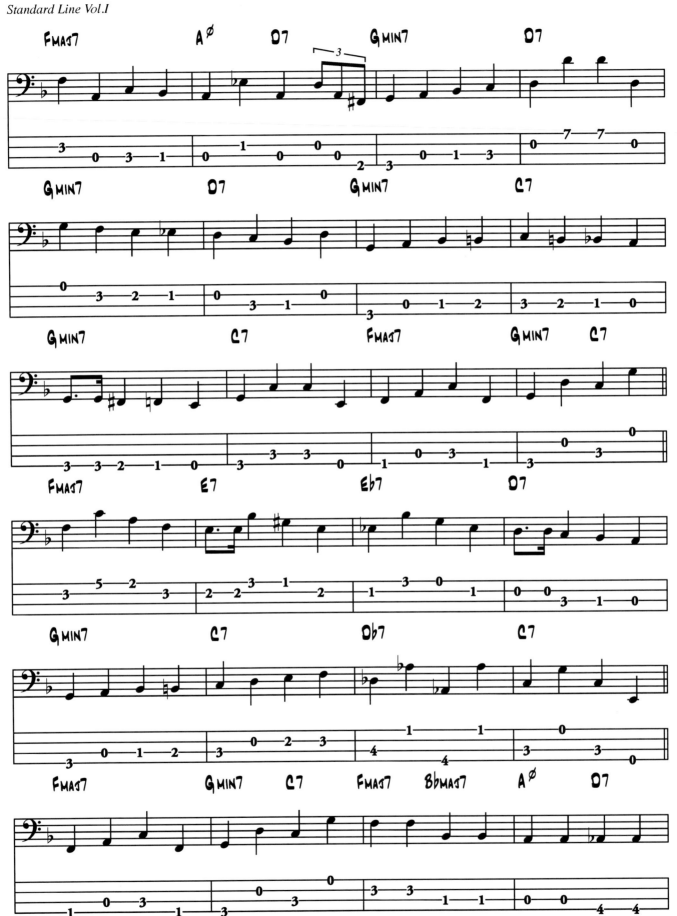

127

129

©Waterfall Publishing House 2011

THE MIXOLYDIAN BEBOP SCALE

THE ASCENDING MIXOLYDIAN BEBOP SCALE

The Dominant 7th Bebop scale is the Mixolydian scale with a chromatic passing tone between the b7th and the root note. In the example below in the F7 Bebop scale the chromatic passing tone is E natural or the major 7th degree of the scale.

Example 1 The ascending Mixolydian scale 2 octaves.

Notice when we get to the second octave or beat 1 of the 3rd measure the first beat of the bar or the *down beat* is G and the next down beat, beat 3 of the 3rd measure is Bb.

Whats being outlined is G min7.

Example 1 F7 Mixolydian scale ascending 2 octaves, beats 1 & 3 are the down beats.

In example 2 we have the F Mixolydian Bebop scale over 2 octaves ascending.
Notice now by adding the chromatic passing tone E natural or the major 7th degree of the scale we now have stronger forward motion over the extended line.
Now all the down beats contain the chord tones, outlining the harmony very clearly and giving a stronger sense of where the line is going.

F Mixolydian Bebop scale ascending 2 octaves, beats 1 & 3 are the down beats.

THE DESCENDING MIXOLYDIAN BEBOP SCALES.

Example 3 shows the descending F Mixolydian scale over two octaves.

Notice when we get to the second octave or beat 1 of the 3rd measure the first beat of the bar or the *down beat* is Eb and the next down beat, beat 3 of the 3rd measure is C.

Whats being outlined by the down beats is Eb 6, or C min7.

Example 3 F Mixolydian scale descending 2 octaves, beats 1 & 3 are the down beats.

In example 4 we have the F Mixolydian Bebop scale over 2 octaves descending.
Notice now by adding the chromatic passing tone E natural or the major 7th degree of the scale we now have stronger forward motion over the extended line.
Now all the down beats contain the chord tones, outlining the harmony very clearly and giving a stronger sense of where the line is going.
Notice on beats 1 and 3 in measures 3 and 4 we now have F, Eb, C, A, clearly outlining the F7 tonality.

Example 4 F Mixolydian Bebop scale descending 2 octaves, beats 1 & 3 are the down beats.

In the next example we look at " WHO'S GLOVE " jazz chord progression # 13 and apply the use of the Mixolydian Bebop scale when constructing our bass line.

" WHO'S GLOVE ? "   Jazz chord progression # 13

APPLYING THE MIXOLYDIAN BEBOP SCALE TO
CONSTRUCTING JAZZ BASS LINES

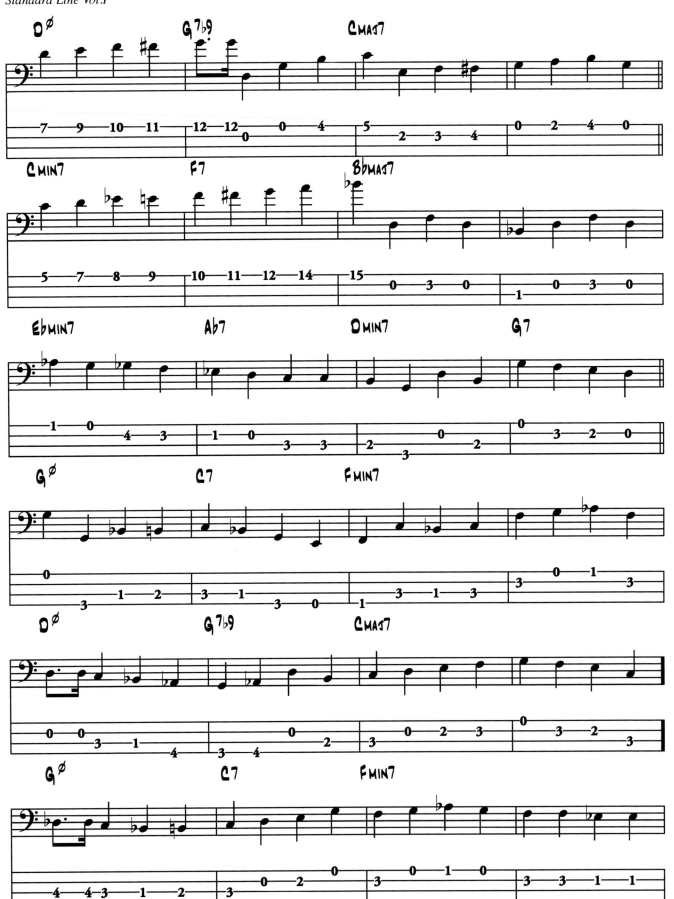

135

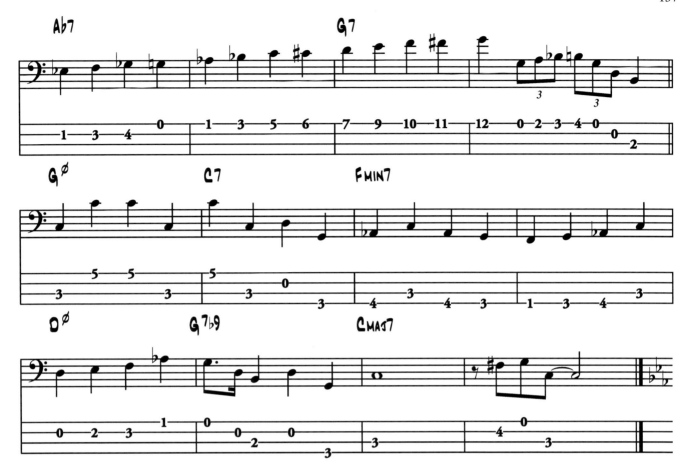

PART IV   JAZZ BASS LINE EXAMPLES OVER STANDARD JAZZ CHORD PROGRESSIONS

" OCEAN ST "

Standard Line Vol.I

143

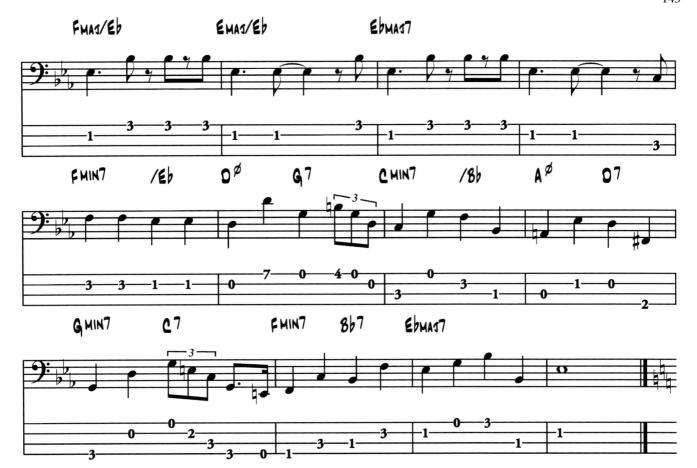

" SLIPPED INTO THE STREAM " Jazz chord progression # 15

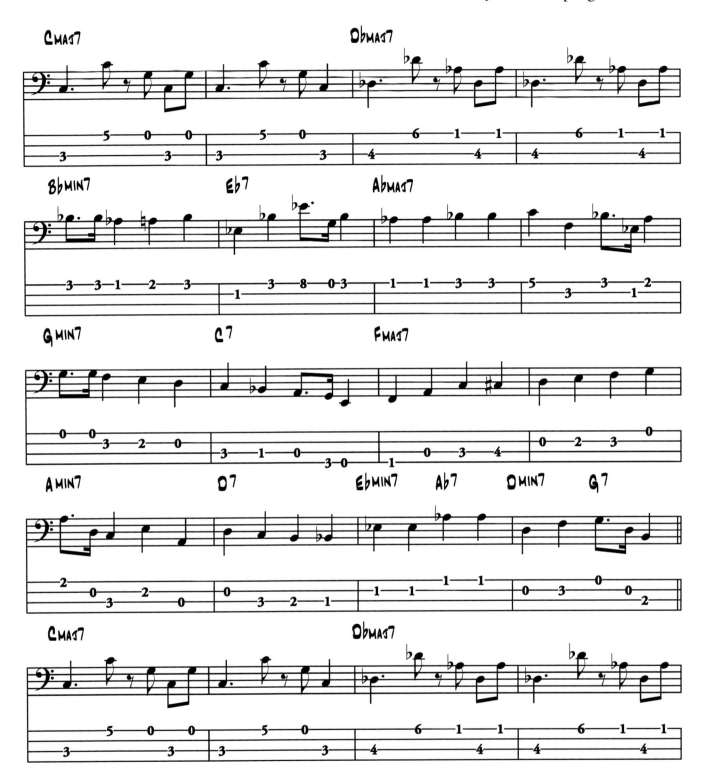

Standard Line Vol.I

" ONLY YOU "

Jazz chord progression # 16

153

155

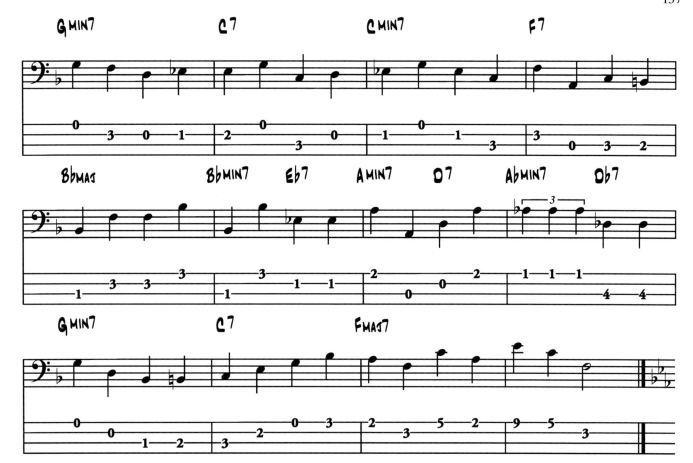

© Waterfall Publishing House 2011

" THE ONE IN GLOVES "   Jazz chord progression # 17

" GARDEN HOSES "   Jazz chord progression # 18

"WHO ARE YOU ?"   Jazz chord progression # 19

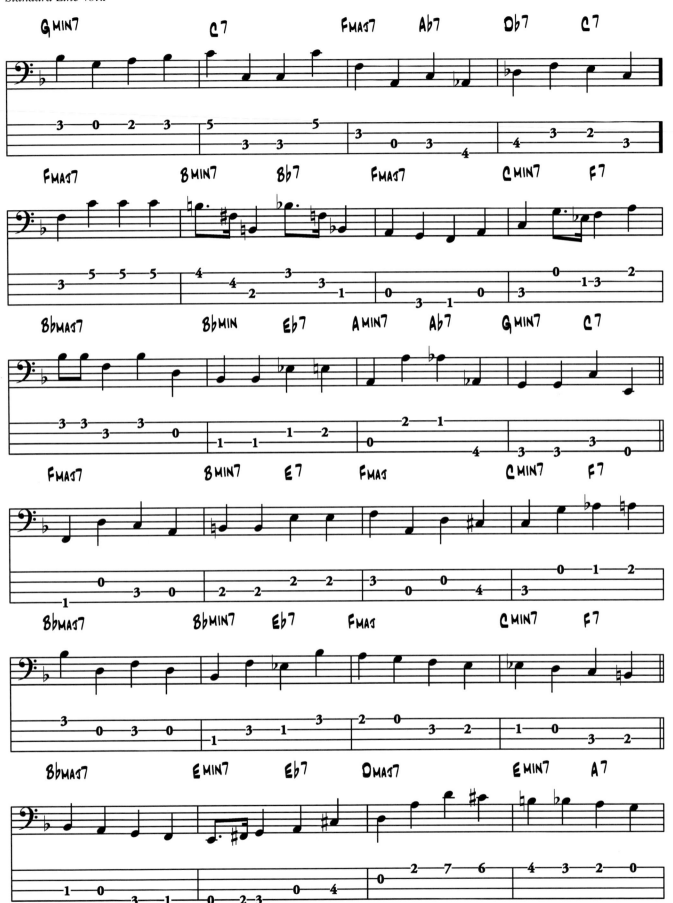

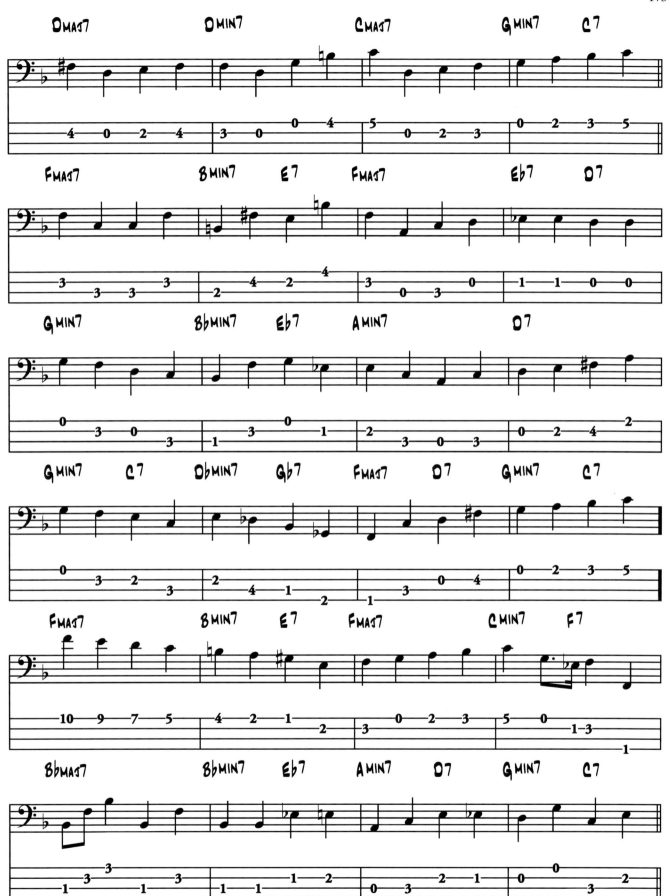

" IDIOSYNCRASY "   Jazz chord progression # 20

Standard Line Vol.I

" THE THIRD "

Jazz chord progression # 21

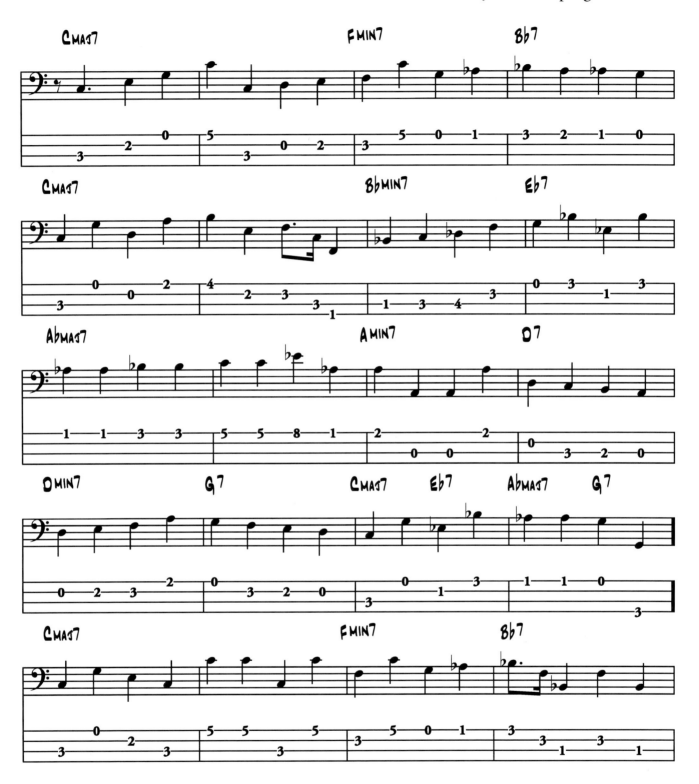

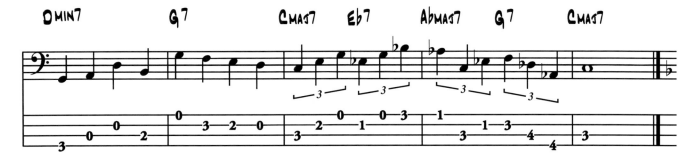

" NEW GLOVES "   Jazz chord progression # 22

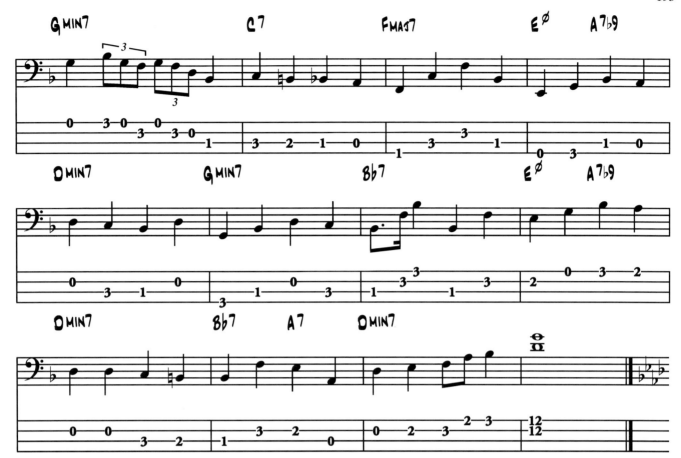

" BRING YOUR STRINGS "   Jazz chord progression # 23

Standard Line Vol.I

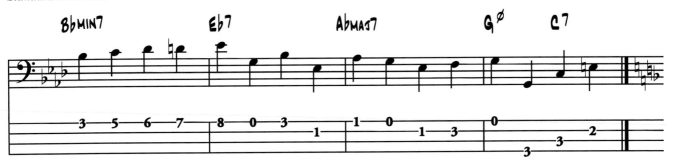

" NO ONES HERE "   Jazz chord progression # 24

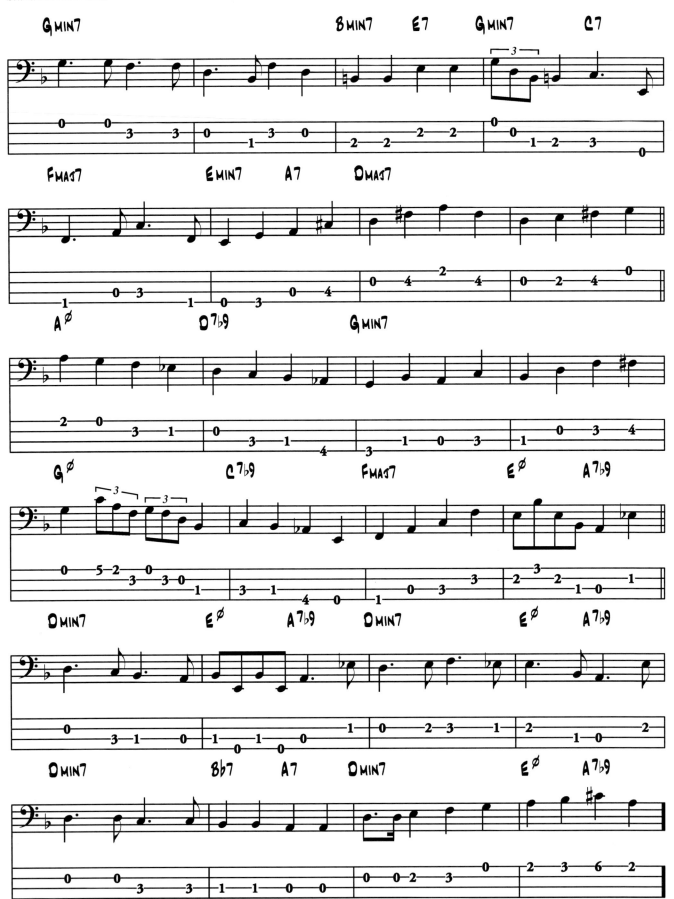

205

©Waterfall Publishing House 2011

IN CONCLUSION ......

It has been a vast amount of work and dedicated practice that brings the bassist to the last page of this book having covered all the examples within.

It has been the aim of this book to give the aspiring bassist a solid grounding in understanding how to construct walking jazz bass lines and support a melody and or soloist.

Having covered the material in this book you are now well on your way to finding your own voice as a bassist and as a jazz musician.

Listen to as much music as you can, Listen to the masters.

NB. This book is designed to make the student familiar with reading and understanding chord symbols in a jazz context, therefore the use of enharmonics is applied.

The objective has been to make the material for the student as easy to absorb as possible, as a confidance building mechanism.

Your thoughts and comments are important to us and assist us in providing future generations of musicians with quality educational material.

Please send youre thoughts or comments to constructwalkingjazzbasslines@gmail.com

Other books available in this series

PRINT EDITIONS

" Constructing Walking Jazz Bass Lines " Book I
Walking Bass Lines : The Blues in 12 Keys

" Constructing Walking Jazz Bass Lines " Book II
Walking Bass Lines : Rhythm Changes in 12 keys

" Constructing Walking Jazz Bass Lines " Book III
Walking Bass Lines : Standard Lines

" Constructing Walking Jazz Bass Lines " Book IV
 - coming soon

Bass Tablature Series

" Constructing Walking Jazz Bass Lines " Book I
Walking Bass Lines : The Blues in 12 Keys -Bass TAB Edition

" Constructing Walking Jazz Bass Lines " Book II
Walking Bass Lines : Rhythm Changes in 12 Keys - Bass TAB Edition

" Constructing Walking Jazz Bass Lines " Book III
Walking Bass Lines : Standard Lines - Bass TAB Edition

" Constructing Walking Jazz Bass Lines " Book IV
Bass Tab Edition - coming soon

E-BOOK EDITIONS

" Constructing Walking Jazz Bass Lines " Book I
Walking Bass Lines : The Blues in 12 Keys

"Constructing Walking Jazz Bass Lines " Book II
Walking Bass Lines : Rhythm Changes in 12 keys

" Constructing Walking Jazz Bass Lines " Book III
Walking Bass Lines : Standard Lines

" Constructing Walking Jazz Bass Lines " Book IV
 - coming soon

Bass Tablature Series

" Constructing Walking Jazz Bass Lines " Book I
 Walking Bass Lines : The Blues in 12 Keys -Bass TAB Edition

" Constructing Walking Jazz Bass Lines " Book II
 Walking Bass Lines : Rhythm Changes in 12 Keys - Bass TAB Edition

" Constructing Walking Jazz Bass Lines " Book III
 Walking Bass Lines : Standard Lines - Bass Tab Edition

" Constructing Walking Jazz Bass Lines " Book IV
 Bass Tab Edition - coming soon

Follow us on the web for news and new release updates.

http://waterfallpublishinghouse.com

http://constructingwalkingjazzbasslines.com

http://basstab.net

Waterfall Publishing House is proud to be associated with the Trees for the Future
Organisation. Visit them on the web at www.plant-trees.org .
Waterfall Publishing House will plant 1 tree per book sold in the " Constructing
Walking Jazz Bass Lines " series through the " Trees for the Future " tree planting
program and will match the commitment for a total of 2 trees planted per book sold.

Follow our quarterly progress at Waterfallpublishinghouse.com